Baby's Opposites

Nancy Raines Day

Illustrated by Rebecca Evans

ini Charlesbridge

Asleep.

Awake.

Daybreak!

Off.

On.

Here.

Gone.

Laugh.

Cry.

Hi!

Bye.

Big!

Small.

Tall.

Short.

Smile!

Frown.

One.

Crowd.

Walk.

Run!

All done.

Work.

Play.

Great day!

Push.

Pull.

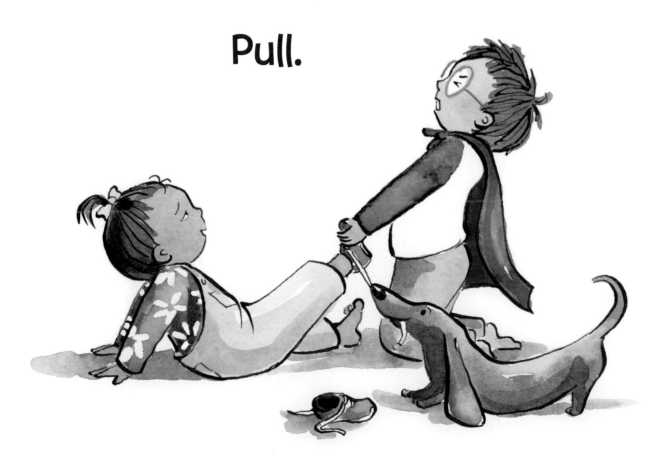

Hungry.

Full.

Warm.

Cold.

Grab hold.

Open.

Dark.

Bright.

Sleep tight!

To Meghan, Neal, and our newest grandson—N. R. D.

For my Lily: you'll always be my baby—R. E.

Text copyright © 2021 by Nancy Raines Day

Illustrations copyright © 2021 by Rebecca Evans

At the time of publication, all URLs printed in this book were accurate and active.
Charlesbridge, the author, and the illustrator are not responsible for the content or accessibility of any website.

Published by Charlesbridge • 9 Galen Street, Watertown, MA 02472
(617) 926-0329
www.charlesbridge.com

Library of Congress Cataloging-in-Publication Data

Names: Day, Nancy Raines, author. | Evans, Rebecca, illustrator.

Title: Baby's opposites / Nancy Raines Day ; illustrated by Rebecca Evans.

Description: Watertown, MA: Charlesbridge, [2021] | Summary: Told in rhyming text, baby and her family experience many opposites
in a busy day that includes enjoying the playground and an ice cream, and ends with a bedtime book and sleep.

Identifiers: LCCN 2019014525 (print) | LCCN 2019020078 (ebook) | ISBN 9781580898782 (reinforced for library use) | ISBN 9781632896971 (ebook)

Subjects: LCSH: Infants—Juvenile fiction. | Polarity—Juvenile fiction. | Stories in rhyme. | Vocabulary. | CYAC: Stories in rhyme. | Babies—Fiction.
English language—Synonyms and antonyms—Fiction. | LCGFT: Stories in rhyme.

Classification: LCC PZ8.3.D3334 Bd 2021 (print) | LCC PZ8.3.D3334 (ebook) | DDC [E]—dc23

LC record available at https://lccn.loc.gov/2019014525

LC ebook record available at https://lccn.loc.gov/2019020078

Printed in China
(hc) 10 9 8 7 6 5 4 3 2 1

Illustrations done in watercolor and ink on Arches 160 lb. hot press paper
Display type set in Snappy Patter by Nick Curtis
Text type set in Billy by David Buck
Color separations by Colourscan Print Co Pte Ltd, Singapore
Printed by 1010 Printing International Limited in Huizhou, Guangdong, China
Production supervision by Jennifer Most Delaney
Designed by Kristen Nobles